RELIGIONS OF HUMA

J 294.5 Rie
33327005218167
Ries, J. (Julien)
Man and the divine in
Hinduism /

D1217751

LIBRARY DISCARD
NON-RETURNABLE

Chelsea House Publishers
1974 Sproul Road, Suite 400
Broomall, PA 19008

The Chelsea House world wide web address is
www.chelseahouse.com

English-language edition
© 2002 by Chelsea House Publishers, a subsidiary
of Haights Cross Communications
All rights reserved.

First Printing

1 3 5 7 9 6 4 2

Left: The temple of Lingaraja in Bhubanesvar, in Orissa state, India. The square bases of the various structures with their different lines become round 'cushions' at the top extremities which end in a point. Multiplicity gives way to unity. The eyes of the pilgrim follow the lines and move towards a single indivisible point. This temple is dedicated to Siva who is represented in the forms of the construction.

Opposite: A 17th-century tempera painting from the Museum of Srinagar, India. It shows a beneficent and resplendent goddess holding a precious vessel, the symbol of the satisfaction of the desires of men.

Library of Congress Cataloging-
in-Publication Data Applied For:
ISBN: 0-7910-6625-8

© 2000 by
Editoriale Jaca Book spa, Milan
All rights reserved.
Originally published by
Editoriale Jaca Book, Milan, Italy

Design by Jaca Book

Original French text by
Julien Ries

JULIEN RIES

MAN AND THE DIVINE IN
HINDUISM

CHELSEA HOUSE PUBLISHERS
PHILADELPHIA

MOOSE JAW PUBLIC LIBRARY

Cows being led back to their stables by mythic characters with a city in the background. The total effect of the painting is one of peace and well-being. Painted by the school of Kishangarh of 1750, and conserved in the National Museum of Delhi, India.

CONTENTS

INTRODUCTION

Hinduism is the religious belief shared by the great majority of people living in India. In order to understand Hinduism, one must start with the ideas and cultural concepts of the Aryans, the Indo-European invaders who penetrated the valleys of the Indus and Ganges rivers 2,000 years before the modern era. However, it is even more necessary to remember that the oral tradition (or *Veda*) of Hinduism has been transformed over the centuries as a result of contact with non-Vedic cultures rooted in India long before the arrival of the Aryan conquerors.

Hinduism is structured upon a number of constants, which have been described by Indian studies. The essential ideas are:

- The Veda, an oral tradition that preceded written language, is the source of many fundamental notions that provide a structure for the religious and social thoughts over the centuries;
- A cosmic order (*dharma*) that includes the universe, man, and life and whose harmony precludes chaos;
- A cyclic concept of time that signifies a perpetual return;
- A system of castes that has to define the social fabric; and
- A concept of the stages of life and of the techniques by which the spirit is liberated (*yoga*), an idea perhaps inherited from pre-Vedic times.

Vedism ignored temples and images of divinity. Influenced by factors not yet fully determined, at the start of the modern era Hinduism underwent a profound change with a new concept of devotion, *bhakti*. Sacrifice gave way to offering (*puja*) and to prayer before statues and other representations of deities in the temples erected by the believers. Here, the faithful turn to the deity of their choice and bear witness to their love in a context of personal relationships. This emphasis on offering and prayer explains the great popularity of the gods of the *bhakti*, like Vishnu and Krishna. The pietist movement, animated by the warmth of an intensely lived devotion, underwent various changes over the centuries. A number of sects developed from Hinduism, many of which continue to the present day. In the absence of a doctrinal authority, in an evolving religion that conserves and reveres its ancient teachings, one can today study the emergence and roles of numerous founders and reformers.

A woman praying in her house near Geyzing, in western Sikkim, India.

1
MODERN HINDUISM

India and Southeast Asia are home to 700 million Hindus, with millions of others living in regions throughout the world. In India, Hindus make up 82 percent of the population. According to the precepts of the faith, one does not become a Hindu; rather, one is born a Hindu. Hindu society continues to exist in the context of a rich cultural, social, and religious heritage that has existed for four millennia, as regulated by the eternal *dharma* (or order of the cosmos), in which man is integrated.

A rite of adoration, of offering, and a cult of deities, or *puja*, which replaced the Vedic sacrifices, is celebrated daily both in Hindu homes and temples. The number and variety of these temples is indeed impressive, with most in northern

***1.** Ramakrishna may be considered as the refounder of contemporary Hinduism.*
***2.** The great impetus to modern Hinduism and its ability to liberate man by following the path of non-violence came from Gandhi, the father of India's independence which was obtained after the Second World War.*

India dedicated to Shiva, most in the south to Vishnu, and to the various other deities according to different regions. Each displays an exuberant mythology and is adorned by great towers (*gopura*) at the four entrances. Everywhere one encounters small chapels, in the trees or beside walls, and miniature places of prayer can be found in city streets. India is the land of the sacred *par excellence*.

Each morning and evening, long lines of believers make their way to the temples to place flowers and other offerings before the statues of the deities. Pilgrimages wend their way toward the thousands of sanctuaries and holy places. During their festivals, a statue of the honored deity is carried on a huge cart, adorned with flowers and pulled by dozens of believers. Prayers, litanies, hymns, music, and cries of joy mark the solemnity.

***3.** A Hindu prostrating himself on the path of the sacred river of Mahanadi, during the Festival of the Sun in Uttar Pradesh, India.*

Everyone lives among the permanent signs of purification: water courses, lakes, and rivers are all considered sacred. At Benares at sunrise, the crowd immerses itself in the sacred waters of the Ganges, while on its banks the rite of cremation for the dead is marked by the casting of ashes

into the river. In Hindu belief, the cow is the symbol of Mother Earth, the one who nourishes mankind, and is therefore considered sacred.

A disciple of Ramakrishna, Vivekananda (1862-1902) created the Hindu mission, a religious order of *swamis*, who serve as community leaders committed to teaching religious doctrine and to organizing displays of solidarity. Hinduism therefore has became a missionary movement with both religious and social aspects. Mohandas Gandhi (1869-1948) sought the total freedom of India from English rule by basing his actions on two principles: the embracing of truth (*satyagraha*) and non-violence (*ahimsa*). Through his efforts, he rehabilitated the lower castes and obtained independence for India.

4. A bus collecting the faithful to take them to Gaumukh, 'The Mouth of the Cow,' where there are the sources of the Ganges, at an altitude of 3861 meters, near Mount Gangotri in the Himalayas. Garhwal district, Uttar Pradesh, India.
5. A priest holds the holy fire as pilgrims bathe during the Festival of Khumba which is held every twelve years at Hardwar, in Garhwal, India.
6. A Hindu prays in a temple dedicated to Shiva in Geyzing, western Sikkim, India.

2
PRE-VEDIC RELIGION

In 1922, the first evidence of a magnificent Bronze-Age civilization that flourished between 2500 and 1700 B.C. was discovered, first in a valley of the Indus and later in Pakistan and in other places in India. To date, 300 sites have been identified. This civilization is known as Pre-Vedic, Hindusian, or as Mohenjo-Daro and Harappa, after the names of its two major archeological sites. The excavations of Mundigak and Mehrgarh have shown that this urban civilization was preceded by a Neolithic agricultural culture dating back to 7000 B.C. Scholars today have more than 3,500 inscriptions that they have not yet been able to decipher, even though there appear to have been many contacts between India and Mesopotamia.

1. 2. 3. 4. Steatite seals showing positive and negative forms of a unicorn and a bull, mythic animals of Hindu civilization. The writing has not yet been deciphered.

The religious documentation found in these sites is important and includes many figurines, many depicting female forms and hundreds of signs or personal seals. These latter were used to authenticate objects, to show ownership, and to place them under the protection of the deities. Many of the seals show a crowned three-faced horned god seated on a throne like a *yogin*, with animals turned toward him. It is believed that this is a prototype of the god Shiva, lord of the animals and prince of yoga.

The many female figurines cause one to think of a Great Goddess. One seal, found at Mohenjo-Daro, shows her between two branches of an Indian *pipal* tree, which today remains a symbol of maternity. She is crowned and is seen escorted by seven young women. It is the Mother Goddess, already represented in Mesopotamia in the tenth millennium, and is indicative of a matriarchal society orientated toward life.

Among the other details of the findings, particular reference should be made to the importance of animalist art, the familiarity of animals with the divine, the importance of the sacred tree, and the cemetery at Harappa with various grave goods testifying to a belief in an ultra-terrestrial existence.

5. The famous steatite seal found at Mohenjo-Daro showing a goddess with a head-dress and many bracelets in the branches of a sacred tree. A man is prostrating himself in a gesture of prayer and offering; he is followed by a goat-like creature with a human head. Lower down there is a procession of seven female figures. It is a scene showing a very ancient ritual.
6. The very well-known limestone sculpture found at Mohenjo-Daro which is thought to represent a city dignitary.
7. Map indicating the main centers of the ancient civilization of the Indus. Today almost the entire area lies in Pakistan.
8. A female idol of the ancient civilization of the Indus. This terracotta figurine was discovered in the city of Harappa and today lies in the Museum Guimet in Paris.

Harappa •

Jhelum

Chenab

Ravi

Sutlej

Indus River

6

• Mehrgarh

Mohenjo-Daro •

• Kot Dijī

• Chanu-Darō

Amrī •

Indus

Hab

• Balakot

Desalpur •

Surkotada •

ARABIAN SEA

7

8

11

THE SPREAD OF HINDUISM

1. *In the second millennium* B.C., *peoples who are today called Indo-European came from the lands north of the Black Sea to the valleys of the Indus and of the Ganges (shown in red in the map) and settled there permanently, introducing a new culture. These newcomers, who*

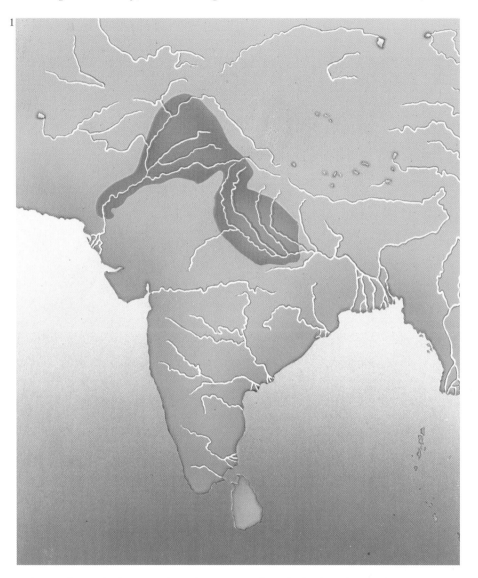

brought with them Vedic ideas, mixed with the local population, forming the nucleus of Hindu culture and religion.

2. *The island of Elephanta in the Indian Ocean, right across from Bombay, is considered as the 'doorway to India' by westerners. It contains one of the most important rupestral temples dedicated to Shiva.*

3. *The entrance to one of the halls excavated in the rock and supported by columns of the temple of the God Shiva on the island of Elephanta.*

4. *Hinduism expanded eastwards from India, first to Sri Lanka and then to south-east Asia all the way to Indonesia. In the 8th and 9th centuries* A.D., *an important Hindu kingdom developed on the island of Java, where the remains of the great temple of Prambanan, the famous capital of the kingdom, can still be admired today.*

5. *Hinduism is present in INDIA—the religion's cradle—where 650 million (82% of the entire population in 1982) profess the faith. Other countries with Hindu minorities are GUYANA and MAURITIUS (25% of the population); BHUTAN, BANGLADESH, and SRI LANKA (10%); PAKISTAN, BURMA, MALAYSIA, INDONESIA, SOUTH AFRICA, SEYCHELLES, and FRENCH GUYANA (1%-2%). Other small groups are to be found in the UNITED KINGDOM and the NETHERLANDS. (Sources: Joanne O'Brien, Martin Palmer, Atlas des Religions dans le Monde, Myriad, London/Autrement, Paris, 1994. Le Monde au Présent II, Encyclopaedia Universalis, Paris 1994).*

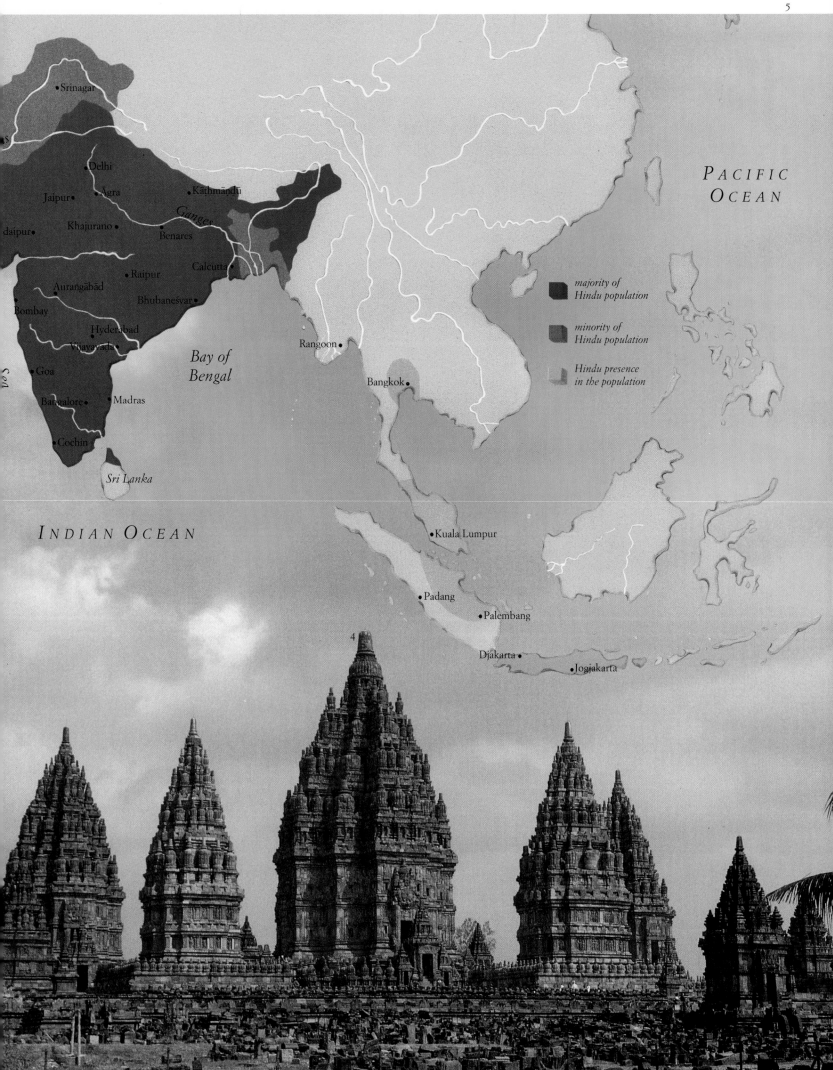

PACIFIC
OCEAN

• Srinagar

• Delhi
Jaipur •   • Āgra   • Kāthmāndū
daipur • Khajurano •   *Ganges*
                  • Benares
                  Calcutta •
          • Raipur
Aurangābād •
          Bhubaneśvar •
Bombay •
          • Hyderabad
Vijayavada •
• Goa   • Rangoon
Bangalore •   • Madras   Bay of
                              Bengal
• Cochin
                              Bangkok •
        Sri Lanka

*majority of
Hindu population*

*minority of
Hindu population*

*Hindu presence
in the population*

INDIAN OCEAN

                    • Kuala Lumpur

                    • Padang
                         • Palembang

4   Djakarta •
                              • Jogjakarta

4
THE VEDA—PRAISE AND CULT OF THE GODS

Toward 1900 B.C., some Aryans from central Asia and the Caucasus made their way into India, advancing slowly with their herds through the Indus and Ganges valleys. They brought with them an oral and spiritual tradition, Veda, representing an eternal law, *sanatana dharma*. By the time this law was written down in 1800 B.C., the Aryan travelers had occupied all of India. No archaeological remains of this period have as yet been discovered.

The Vedas are the most ancient Aryan religious texts of India and consist of four collections. The RIG VEDA consists of 1,017 hymns in honor of the 33 deities, to whom the faithful offer praise, invitations to share in sacrifices, and prayers for protection, happiness, and salvation. The SAMA VEDA is a collection of melodies and chants used during the celebrations that reaffirm the faith. The YAJUR VEDA, intended for priests, is a record of the rituals, especially those concerning the seasonal sacrifices for agricultural work and for harvest. The ATHARVA VEDA, the veda of the magic formulas, consists of spells and elements of popular cults, combined with later reflections.

As in Aryan society, the spiritual world is divided into three groups according to function. The sovereign gods, Mitra-Varuna, are the gods of the sacred, of the cosmos, and of the universal rule (*rita*)—assuring maintenance of the cosmic order. Indra and his Maruts, representing the second group, are the gods of war and conquest and serve as the guardians against enemies. The third group includes the Ashvin or Nasatya, young gods who are believed to travel throughout the heavens daily and who play an indispensable role in fertility. Agni is the god of fire, a divine power, and messenger of the gods; 200 vedic hymns are dedicated to him. The *soma*, the finest offering that can be made to a deity, consists of the drinking of an intoxicating liquid made from a local plant, symbolizing life. The entire religion consists of cultic and utilitarian practices, with the gods in the service of men. Predominantly a patriarchal belief system, the Veda has few feminine deities.

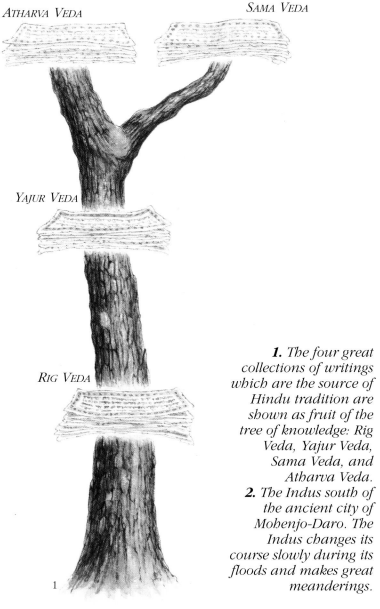

ATHARVA VEDA

SAMA VEDA

YAJUR VEDA

RIG VEDA

1

1. *The four great collections of writings which are the source of Hindu tradition are shown as fruit of the tree of knowledge: Rig Veda, Yajur Veda, Sama Veda, and Atharva Veda.*
2. *The Indus south of the ancient city of Mohenjo-Daro. The Indus changes its course slowly during its floods and makes great meanderings.*

2

3. Agni is the god of fire and one of the oldest Indian deities. He can be recognized by means of the burning crown he wears on his head.
4. Indra is the god of thunder and of rain. He brings water and life, but he has also been venerated as the god of lightning bolts and of war.

5. Varuna, the god who created the universe, is described in the Vedic texts as the god of the heavens and earth. Nowadays he is venerated as the god of the waters.
6. Shiva, here shown in an 8th-century bronze bust, is the supreme deity for his followers.

7. The Ganges in ancient times, at the time of the coming of the first Hindus. The Indo-Europeans arrived on the banks of the river and became farmers and shepherds, utilizing the river as a great means of communication. They also began to venerate the river as a place of purification.

5
THE BRAHMANA: SALVATION THROUGH SACRIFICE

By around 800 B.C., the Aryans were organized into four basic social classes (*varna*). The *Brahmins*, the dominant class, had the monopoly of the Vedas, the sacred, and the cults. The *Kshatriyas*, noblemen and warriors, ruled over society. The *Vaishyas*, agriculturists and craftsmen, produced society's wealth. The *Shudras*, non-Aryan servants, were excluded from the Vedic rituals.

Conscious of their own dignity, the *Brahmins* recorded the passages and commentaries of the Vedas, or Brahmana, texts which deal with rites of sacrifice. From a Vedic belief in the gods, they pass to the mysticism of sacrifice, which becomes a sort of clockwork movement regulating the progress of the universe.

During this time, Brahma-Prajapati emerged a new god, Lord of all creatures, a primordial being whose word is a creative force (*vac*). He is time, the year, and the sacrifice, the all and the fullness. Tribute to Brahma-Prajapati occurs on the site of an excavated pit, where a high altar is built and on which the sacred fire, or Agni, is placed. The five courses of bricks placed here represent the five worlds, the five seasons, the five cardinal points. Atop a heap of wood is placed a lotus leaf, which symbolizes the earth; a golden lamina, which symbolizes immortality; and, finally, a statue of a man represent-

1. The Indo-Europeans who settled in India developed four social classes, known as varna. The Brahmins **(b)** are the priests who look after the relationship of the community with the sacred on behalf of the entire community.

They look after the Vedas and take care to pass them to succeeding generations. The Kshatriya **(a)** have military power and they form groups, each one headed by a raja or monarch, who is here shown seated on a throne. The Vaishya **(c)** have the economic power since they are the cultivators and the

*breeders, which produce the later trade. To each class is attributed a deter-mined color which is distinctive characteristic: the Brahmins are allotted the white color, the Kshatriya red, and the Vaishya yellow if they are merchants or blue if they are farmers. The last class, that composed of non-Aryans, is that of the Shudra **(d)**, the servants.*
2. *The illustration shows the three fires of sacrifice. In the foreground there is the fire of south that functions as a guard, on the left that of the master of the house, and on the right the fire of the offerings with the priests.*

ing Prajapati. Agni (the sacred fire) serves as the immolator. Such sacrifice through fire is believed to grant entrance to immortality, giving this ritual great importance.

Three fires are lit for every sacrifice: the *garhapatya*, the fire of the mas-ter of the house who offers the sacrifice; the *ahavaniya*, the fire of the offerings, which carries the gifts to the gods; and the *dakshinagni*, the fire of the south, which stands guard over the ritual. Central to the consecra-tion is the idea of faith, *shraddha*. By means of the sacrifice, man is believed born a second time, with the third birth occurring with the fire of cremation.

The sacrifice became the basis of the three Aryan social classes since the ideology corresponded to the theology. The members of the three classes are called upon to pass though four stages of life: first as disciples of a guru, then as masters of a house (*grihasthin*). Subsequently they retire with their brides to become inhabitants of the forest (*vanaprasthin*). Finally they extinguish every fire and renounce all worldly things, living as hermits (*samnyasin*).

2

6
THE UPANISHADS

Derived from the words *Upa ni sad*, or 'sitting beside,' the Upanishads are sacred texts that emerged between 800 and 600 B.C., each having its own doctrine of initiation, as communicated by a guru. The Upanishads impart to the faithful secret knowledge about the nature of sacrifice, the divine, the cosmos, the nature of life and death, and the path of salvation by means of gnosis (higher-knowledge).

As new doctrines emerged, mention is made of Brahman, who, on a higher spiritual level, is the Absolute and is represented by a divine character, Brahma. *Atman* is the eternal and immortal principle that animates the individual, moving one toward spiritual growth and, ultimately, salvation. In the Upanishads, the *atman* is called upon to liberate the individual spirit from the body, thus achieving the perfect identity with Brahman and so leading one to salvation, or *moksha*. *Samsara* (as opposed to *moksha*) is the passage from one existence to another. The *karman* is an invincible force that fuels a continuing cycle of rebirth, so that the fruits of one's actions unrealized in one lifetime may be realized through

1

2

successive rebirths. Thus, one's actions in this life are believed to determine his or her role in the next, making the concept of *karman* central to the idea of retribution. In accordance with this belief, transmigration (death and rebirth) will continue to occur until the karmic force is exhausted.

Upanishad Brahmanism emphasizes a double doctrine: first, *brahman-atman*, or salvation via the search for identity through ecstatic experiences; and second, *karman-samsara*, or the influence of one's acts on the chain of existence, on spiritual liberation, and on salvation. The *atman* makes man an immortal being who reaches Brahman through an ecstatic experience. Because man remains free to act, his future existence will depend on his choices, with every good action moving him toward salvation. In so far as man acts in accordance with the *dharma*, he will change the world. Thus the Upanishads describe an ethic of moral responsibility. Ecstasy dissipates the power of the *karman*, thus obstructing transmigration and bringing about the conjunction of the *atman* with Brahman, finally bringing man into the realm of the divine.

1. In a night with a full moon, particularly favorable to sacred ceremonies, a procession of women makes its way to a temple in the midst of a forest. A brahmin sits in front of the temple; as its custodian he has the duty to officiate over its rites. Farther away two hermits sit in meditation on the threshold of the grottoes where they live. Beyond the forest one can see the classical Indian village on the banks of a river.
2. A hermit.

7
YOGA AND ITS TECHNIQUES OF SALVATION

The word Yoga is derived from *yug*, meaning 'to tie' or 'to unite.' With origins that date back to pre-Vedic India, the term is used by all the forms of knowledge and religions of the Vedas, and also by Buddhism, to the present day. Yoga can only be learned through the help of a guru who can be Ishvara, the pure divine spirit, the ideal of the *yogin* and the *yogini*.

Yoga is based on the theory that man is composed of both matter (*prakriti*) and spirit (*puruhsa*). To detach one's spirit from the material, one needs a deep knowledge that can overcome all ignorance and a progressive practice of liberation.

The *yogin* must begin on this journey of spiritual liberation by living in accordance with ten virtues: the respect for all living creatures (*ahimsa*); the respect for truth (*satya*); the respect for property (*asteya*); the respect for chastity (*brahmacarya*); a poor life; a morality of purity; a strength of spirit; the absence of personal ambition; entrance into the cult of a divinity; and the thirst for knowledge.

The techniques consist of complex exercises, which are simultaneously physical, spiritual, and moral, and which include the disciplines of breathing, concentration, and meditation. Various methods for liberation have been proposed over the centuries: the *karma-yoga*, by means of free action without the expectation of recompense; the *bhakti-yoga* by means of adoration and mystic love; the *hatha-yoga*, very well known in the West, by means of physical exercise; the *mantra-yoga* by means of the chanting and prayer; and the *jnana-yoga*, by means of gnosis or a superior knowledge.

These various techniques seek to give the *yogin* a path of liberty by freeing him from the material concerns of daily life, from the empty waste of time; and from the dispersion of his spiritual powers. Through discipline and the rhythm of respiration, he will define his consciousness and his thoughts; through concentration, multiplicity and fragmentation are abolished and unity is achieved. In this way the *yogin* raises himself to a superior level and may experience spiritual liberation while still living in the material universe.

1. A yogin in a typical position.
2. In a park in a modern city, a master yogin is teaching students how to control their breathing. Every position and movement in yoga must start from a proper breathing technique.

BHAKTI—THE RELIGION OF SALVATION

At around 500 B.C., the devout Hindu begins to place his trust in a personal god, a beloved deity able to return this love. Derived from the word *bhaj* meaning 'to share,' this new form of devotion is called *bhakti*: it is a fervent and tender practice allowing the faithful to receive the love of the god whom he or she adores. Vedism did not make use of temples and statues, while Brahmanism offered sacrifices and *puja*. With the emergence of *bhakti*, many temples were constructed, and India filled with sacred images. Women participated enthusiastically in this popular fervor because they wanted to see the face of their god and to offer him tribute (often in the form of flowers and fruit). Thus by surpassing Vedism and Brahmanism, the Hindu religion assumed a new aspect, for the first time providing the believer (*bhakta*) with a loving god who loved him in return.

Vishnu became a supreme god, a Bhagavan, a Gracious Lord who appears on earth every time that sacred order (*dharma*) is threatened. As the popular deity who safeguarded the cosmos, Vishnu elicited great devotion, with many temples dedicated to him. The myths of his ten *avatara*—that is, 'incarnations' or descents to earth—were staged, recounted, put to music, and celebrated, constituting the Vishnuite sacred liturgy. Among his forms, Vishnu became a fish to save the first man from the flood, a tortoise to give origin to the animals, and man-lion to combat demons. At the end of the world it is believed that he will become Kalki, the white horse. Growing steadily in popularity and power, the rich mythology of Vishnu celebrated a god who was close to man and served as the custodian of the world, eventually becoming a hero to supplant the Brahmins, Rama, then Krishna, and finally Buddha.

Another important *bhakti* god is Shiva, the lord of life and death, the creator, destroyer, and re-creator of the cosmos. (It should be noted that unlike many Western religions, Hinduism supports the idea of cyclic time, in which birth and death, creation and re-creation are constantly recurring facets of existence.) In art, Shiva is depicted with three heads, representing his threefold role as the creator of the cosmos, its keeper, and its destroyer. He also has three eyes, the third centered on his forehead, representing the eye of knowledge. The cult of Shiva is a fertility cult that probably derives from Mohenjo-Daro and whose devotion centers upon the adoration of the *linga*, a cylindrical stone that serves as the symbol of both creation and fertility. Originally not as popular as Vishnu, Shiva has made great progress over the centuries, with the many Shivaite sects currently enjoying great popularity in India.

2. A poet praying to Vishnu. Miniature from 1730. Chandigarh Museum, India. The acts of man, neither the smallest nor the greatest, are worth nothing without devotion.

1. Vishnu Surya who represents the Rising Sun. A statue from the temple of Konarak, at Orissa in India, which is dedicated to the Rising Sun.

3. A monumental statue of the god Shiva with his three heads from the temple at Elephanta, India. The head in the middle represents the creative aspect of the god, that on the right his protective aspect, while that on the left the destructive aspect.
4. The caption is to be found on p. 24.

THE *BHAGAVAD GITA—* "THE CELESTIAL SONG"

1

Preceding page:
4. At Ellora, on the high plains of Deccan in India, there are numerous rupestral temples. Probably the most famous is the Kailasa, that is the mountain or, better, the paradise of Shiva. It is not actually a construction but a temple excavated in the rock, sculpted, and hollowed inside. The pilgrim enters in the square sanctuary, the roof of which is shown on the top left corner, then into a hall of which one can see the lotus-shaped roof with four lions, and finally in the important principal sanctuary which is shown from the outside.

2

The *Bhagavad Gita* (the Song of the Lord), analogous to the Bible in India and the best known book of its religious literature, consists of a dialogue between the god Krishna and his faithful Arjuna. Inserted in the sixth book of the Mahabharata, one of the great sagas, it is considered as a sacred document, a sort of 'Krishna's gospel,' describing the third god of the *bhakti* who reveals himself as Bhagavan, the Supreme Lord, and dictates the behavior expected of his faithful, the *bhakta* Arjuna.

The *Gita* unifies the previous doctrines and mystical teachings in a harmonious synthesis. It describes the first path of salvation, the *karma-marga*, the path of actions, but goes beyond it by teaching about the action done according to duty (*dharma*) without seeking recompense. It mentions the path of knowledge pre-announced in the Upanishads, *jnana-marga*, but transforms it and leads the believer to the Bhagavan, the supreme being superior to the Brahman. It pro-

claims the indispensability of the path of devotion and of love (*bhakti-marga*), which is the path of the abandonment of oneself to Bhagavan Krishna, a personal god. In this belief system, the individual may act freely, but always with reference to Krishna who is the creator of the world and who will thus conclude his cycle.

The revelation of the *Gita* must be seen as part of the mythic vision of the epic poem, which presents a struggle and where man achieves salvation as a result of the obedience of the *bhakta* to the Bhagavan, through his devotion to Krishna.

It is believed that the wheel of the *samsara* will finally stop for those who show their devotion to Krishna through their love and who entrust all their actions to their god. This will mark their escape from the cycle of rebirth, as a result of the psychological help of the Bhagavan who supports their efforts, removes the deceptive veil of illusion, and reveals himself to his believers, in accordance with the strict interpretation of Hinduism.

1. Krishna playing the flute.

2. The encounter between the mythic Radha, who is followed by a servant girl, and Krishna who sits in a copse is soberly represented in a 1730 miniature. The love for the god is an experience that brings joy on earth.

3. A scene from the Bhagavad Gita showing the god Krishna driving the chariot of Arjuna the warrior while he gives him instructions on how to become a perfect Hindu.

4. A detail from the temple of Vishnu Surya Rising Sun at Konarak, Orissa, India. It shows the rear part of the chariot being pulled towards the sun.

LIBERATION THROUGH THE DEVOTION TO KRISHNA

BHAGAVAD GITA

The Lord says:

VI, 47. *Whoever among all the yogin remains in me and, full of faith, adores me from the deepest of his soul will be deemed by me as having achieved the apex of the yogic union.*

VIII, 5. *Whoever, remembering me in his last moments, abandons his mortal body and leaves, will have access to my being; there is no doubt at all about this.*

VIII, 7. *Remember me at all times and fight, with your mind and your judgment oriented toward me. And you will come to me without any doubt.*

XII, 6. *Those who place all their actions in me, who have no other pleasure but me and who adore me and gather all their thoughts in me by means of an exclusive discipline, for them I will be the one who will immediately pluck them from the ocean of transmigration and of death...*

The god Krishna, who had his origins in the region of Mathura, has assumed a very important role in Hinduism, owing to the *Bhagavad Gita*, which has strongly influenced Indian thinking for more than two millennia. The doctrine of the *karman*, stating the influence of one's acts on transmigration, and that of salvation, which is liberation from the rebirth cycle, have undergone deep changes.

The above extracts demonstrate the new orientation toward salvation. The relationship of love between the believer and Krishna during one's life realizes the ideals of yoga to the highest degree. This orientation will be a permanent invocation to Krishna during the life of the *bhakta*. At the moment of a devotee's death, it is believed that Krishna will terminate his rebirth cycle. These texts show the importance of the union between god and the individual (achieved through the *bhakti*) and provide a personal link between man and divinity.

1. A swami follower of Krishna mediating and studying in his ashrama (hermitage) in Gangotri, in the district of Garhwal, Uttar Pradesh, India.
2. A popular picture of the city of Mathura in Uttar Pradesh, the destination of pilgrimages to Krishna, showing the pilgrims' route. The entire circuit of the city is made by passing through the woods and the parks. The pictures around the border show episodes from the life of Krishna: the marriage of his parents, the apparition of Vishnu, the newly-born babe being carried to his adoptive family, his education, his pranks, his adventures, and so on.

GLOSSARY

words in CAPITALS *are cross references*

ahimsa 'absence of the desire to kill.' This doctrine of nonviolence inspires an absolute respect toward all living creatures. It first appeared about the sixth century B.C. in Hinduism and was adopted by Buddhism and Jainism.

Aranyaka 'of the forest.' The name given to a group of 'forest texts,' written by Vedic hermits, probably at the end of the BRAHMANA period.

Atman The name given to the eternal principle that gives life to the individual; 'the self,' 'the personal soul,' the substratum of the subconscious. Many Hindu texts expound the Brahmanic ideas about the *atman*, the principle of life, the central power of man, he immortal spiritual principle. Buddhism opposed this doctrine.

Bhagavad Gita 'The song of the Lord.' A poem that comprises the sixth book of the Mahabharata. This 'Indian Bible' consists of a dialogue between KRISHNA and his faithful follower, Arjuna, and emphasizes devotion as the path of salvation. The poem inspired Mahatma Gandhi.

bhakti From *bhaj* 'to divide with others.' A religious philosophy that intends to establish ties of love between the believers and their gods. Known in India since the beginning of our era, *bhakti* has been responsible for great changes in both religious thought and practice, and has made popular the cult of KRISHNA, intensified the cult of Vishnu, and has influenced Buddhism. Indian art has also been greatly influenced by it.

Brahman In its neuter form, the word refers to the ritual formula, then Vedic wisdom, and the knowledge of the Brahmin, the Hindu priest. In its masculine form, the **brahmin** is one of the ministers of the Vedic sacrifice; it also refers to the priest, the spiritual master of society in which case the plural is **brahmins**, the members of the highest caste of Vedic society. **Brahman** with a capital letter refers to the Absolute, the Universal, the Pure Energy, which becomes **Brahma** when it is invoked as a personal god.

Brahmana 'belonging to the brahmins.' In its neuter form, the word refers to a number of texts that make up Vedic revelation. These prose texts were written between 800 and 600 B.C. and describe the celebration of sacrifices (ceremonies, myths, legends).

dharma The cosmic and social order that keeps the universe in existence. Immutably fixed, this order is supported by a synthesis of rules and natural phenomena. The behavior of individuals conditions the proper functioning of the universe and their normal life in the *dharma*. As part of the sacred realm, the *dharma* is looked after by the BRAHMINS.

gopura Towers with a rectangular base which, from the eleventh century, were built in southern India above the entrance to the walled area of a temple. Built with a varying number of floors, each tower progressively narrows as it rises. Each floor is decorated with hundreds of statues of gods and saints.

karman That which provides the basis of the ritual act, its value, and its action. It is an invisible and invincible force that penetrates the soul and starts it on the cycle of rebirth. The doctrine of *karman*, which affirms the necessity of rebirth in order to reap the fruits which had not 'matured' in the present life, has become universally accepted in India.

Krishna A 'black' god, the eighth *avatara* of the god Vishnu, Krishna has become very popular throughout India. His cult originated from Mathura (Uttar Pradesh), a city which has been described as the seat of wisdom and knowledge. He is the god who destroys evil and inspires knowledge. The schools of late Visnhuism consider Krishna as the plenary reincarnation of the Supreme Being. As a god he was responsible for the BHAGAVAD GITA—'the celestial song.'

moksha The final liberation from the cycle of rebirth through union with the BRAHMAN. It represents salvation for the Hindu.

puja A public and private Hindu prayer and sacrifice. It includes a system of rites (and occasionally chants) that vary according to the different regions and times.

purusha 'male,' 'Man.' Masculine spirit, global spirit of humanity, human unit that derives from the VEDA. Cosmic man who gave birth to the universe during a sacrifice celebrated by the gods.

risi 'sages.' Poets and soothsayers of the Vedic era who, according to tradition, composed the hymns of the **Rig Veda** 'knowledge of hymns.' This collection of 1,017 hymns and the oldest Vedic book were imported by the nomadic Indo-European tribes who arrived in India. The *risi* received them as revelations from the gods. These hymns and chants invoke and celebrate the gods.

rita 'natural order of things.' Owing to this order, which is looked after by the god Varuna, and to the inner forces, life is conserved. Every contrary act constitutes a ritual crime that demands expiation.

samsara The infinite cycle of birth and rebirth that conditions life according to the KARMAN of every being according to the merit of the actions performed. The cycle is supported by a law of recompense of one's actions which, on one hand, demands the MOKSHA and, on the other, transmigration.

satyagraha 'fortitude of truth.' It is the spirit of the followers of AHIMSA, non-violence. This movement was launched by Gandhi to obtain independence for India.

shraddha 'faith.' A Vedic form of consecration often considered as a god and that gives its name to the offering made by a BRAHMIN. One of the words of Hindu sacrality.

soma A potion used in Vedic times in the celebration of sacrifices. This intoxicating drink was made from the plant of the same name and was considered holy and able to confer immortality.

swami or **svami** A title of respect given to Hindu philosophers who are considered masters and to the religious.

Upanishads The texts of the Vedic revelation, which show the way of the Absolute and of the liberation from the cycle of rebirth. The oldest date back to the sixth or fifth centuries B.C. The Upanishads announce salvation through the conjunction of the ATMAN with the BRAHMAN. According to the Upanishad, salvation is achieved through mystic knowledge.

varna 'class.' The word refers to a social function, a statute, and one's relationship to the VEDAS. Vedic society was ideally divided into four *varnas*: the BRAHMINS, men dedicated to the sacred; the **Kshatriya**, the warriors who defended society; the **Vaishya** who were farmers, livestock breeders, and tradesmen, who had the duty to feed society; and the **Shudra**, a group composed of non-Aryans who had no access to the Vedas.

Veda 'knowledge.' This is the knowledge of the revelation transmitted through the most ancient sacred texts. Hindus speak of **sanatana dharma**, 'the eternal law,' which has been given to man and which is immutable. The **Rig Veda** consists of a collection of hymns; the **Sama Veda** which contains chants and melodies indispensable for the cult; and the **Yajur Veda**, a collection of sacrificial rites and consists of the ritual of celebration. The **Atharva Veda** brings together magic and gnosis, which is a Greek word meaning 'knowledge,' that is a form of wisdom allowing for salvation.

yoga from *yug*, 'to tie.' A complex of philosophical systems and techniques that teach the means of liberating the spirit restrained by the body. Yoga demands physical, spiritual, and moral training, as well as breathing techniques, concentration, and meditation. The various techniques are ultimately aimed to unify the human spirit and the Universal Principle.

INDEX